Dedication

This booklet is dedicated to my darling wife, Annette, who, despite much pain and many setbacks, stuck with me through thick and thin for over sixty-one years. She died on 13th September 2024 and will be my mainstay forever.

TABLE OF CONTENT

What If Darwin Has Misled The World?

Just a few weeks after the funeral of my dear wife, Annette, and quite out of the blue, my cleaning lady , and friend, startled me by saying "Colin, are you quite sure that you will see Annette again some day?" I replied "absolutely", and this led into a conversation about God.

It is always difficult today to know what is truth and what is going to bring harm to our lives, and she asked me a few more questions. During this conversation, I picked up a small wooden rhinoceros (which my wife and I had purchased many years ago) and said to her, "look at this rhino! That animal is so special! How does its stomach work? How does its brain work? It is totally wonderful, complex and intricate! How was it made? We, as human beings, are even more extraordinary than a creature like that!"

Those few simple words started me thinking about creation, and the amazing world in which we live. Then they inspired me to turn to my computer in order to look for the famous illustration of " the human evolution concept" by Rudolph Zallinger (a scientist and painter in the 1960's) whose picture called "the march of progress" has influenced massively the thinking of every succeeding generation.

It shows figures that purport to outline the evolution of man - from monkey, through various stages, until a male emerges at the end of the line of fifteen, still naked, very hairy, and carrying what looks like a spear. The final figure still seems a bit hairy, but much more like a human male of today.

For simplicity sake, this illustration is abbreviated mostly to show only half a dozen creatures. In the modern day. It has been criticised by several scientists, and is acknowledged to have inconsistencies

Zallinger was influenced by the even more famous book by Charles Darwin called "On the Origin of Species", which was published in 1859, and led many people to doubt the story of creation in the Bible.

To quote "Wikipedia" which states that "it introduced the scientific theory that populations evolve over the course of generations through a process of natural selection. The book presents a body of evidence that the diversity of life arose by common descent through a branching pattern of evolution."

"Wikipedia" also prints a summary of Darwin's theory as:

1) "Every species is fertile enough that, if all offspring survived to reproduce, the population would grow.
2) Despite periodic fluctuations, populations remain roughly the same size.
3) Resources such as food are limited and are relatively stable over time.

4) A struggle for survival ensues.

5) Individuals in a population vary significantly from one another.

6) Much of this variation is heritable.

7) Individuals less suited to the environment are less likely to survive and less likely to reproduce. Individuals more suited to the environment are more likely to survive and more likely to reproduce and leave their heritable traits to future generations, which produces the process of natural selection.

8) This slowly effected process results in populations changing to adapt to their environments, and ultimately, these variations accumulate over time to form new species."

How many of these assertions have been proved to be wrong in the over one hundred and sixty years since Darwin penned his book?

Consider the following:

1. It is acknowledged by most scientists today that, however much the “great British Public” may believe in it so implicitly, “The march of progress” picture mentioned above is ***not*** totally correct.
2. Populations throughout the world have grown hugely since the nineteenth century.
3. It has been possible to grow more food using better methods and a liberal use of fertilisers.
4. With much improved medical practices and medicines, his point (7) is no longer true to any extent. Things also have changed radically since the time of Darwin.

I have other questions for Charles Darwin and his “absolute certainties”, which probably are unanswerable by scientists or ecologists:

How did the "primeval swamp" become such different and utterly lovely creatures as:

- A caterpillar/ butterfly
- A human being
- A squirrel
- Many millions of utterly diverse creatures
- And a snake?

Nowhere in its nearly five hundred scholarly pages does it attempt to answer the following very significant questions:

1. Assuming that the first monkey emerged, where did the second monkey come from?
2. How was it created? If it was born, how did that come about?
3. Otherwise, how did a single monkey become two?
4. Did the monkeys suddenly develop into female as well as male animals?
5. Did they suddenly have a new and strange ability to procreate?
6. When and how did the major (and essential) differences between males and females develop? And why did this happen? Why are men and women physically different, and what (or who) brought about sex and birth?

It is inconceivable that the assumed first monkey (if any) could have survived very long under the terrible conditions, and lack of nourishment which it must certainly have experienced on crawling out of the primeval swamp. It is most unlikely, therefore, that it would live until the age when it could have a baby or babies.

Even today, there are very few hermaphrodites, and most of those must, from time to time, find a member of the opposite sex to continue the species. Monkeys do not fall into that class, anyway! The first monkey, then, would have been either male or female. It is totally unthinkable that both male and female monkeys could crawl at the same time from the primeval swamp (if any). It is, therefore, impossible for more monkeys to be created.

More unanswerable questions are as follows:-

1) **Why does the utterly marvellous world we live in contain everything which every living organism, including human beings, needs to exist and flourish?**
2) **How does this world come to be so truly beautiful and diverse?**
3) **Estimates of the number of species today are as follows:**

   a) About 1050 million insect types
   b) About 12260 reptile species
   c) About 11190 bird species
   d) About 6730 animal species
   e) And there may be about 3.5 trillion fish in the world

How can all these very different species have materialized, even over the millions of years as proposed by scientists and naturalists today?

It MUST have been GOD who brought about these miracles!

How He did it, I, as a mere human being, have no idea, but I DO know (as stated above) that one monkey cannot become two monkeys of different sexes – unless they are created by the Hand of God.

Incidentally, there were certainly both male and female animals on the ark at the time of the “great flood”, which wiped out all land life. The Bible records this!

Last night I was watching a television program in which they were speaking about a great flood which the producers thought had inundated the area around the British Isles about 9000 years ago. How strange is that, when previously scientists had denied that there had been any such an event!

Darwin looked carefully at several species of animal – like dogs and pigeons, and concluded that, because these can change over time (sometimes as a result of human intervention and selective breeding); given the passing of enough time, they will become entirely new species.

BUT: - He himself comments in chapter 4 of his book, "On the Origin of Species", thus:

"Can we wonder, then, that Nature's productions should be far "truer" in character than man's productions; that these should be infinitely better adapted to the most complex conditions of life, and should plainly bear the stamp of far higher workmanship"? Does this statement mean that he still believes in God as creator?

I have no problem with accepting that animals/plants change and modify over long periods, BUT, to me, where they came from in the first place is not changeable. Dogs still remain dogs, pigeons remain pigeons, and sheep and cattle do not change into another species. All of these are still distinct and separate animals or birds; some bred with different characteristics to others.

Even though it may be true that some new varieties of animals have been produced by selective breeding, this fact is dwarfed by the amazing bird, insect and fish populations of the world.

Once again, how is it possible that the utter diversity of plant and animal life emerged from a lifeless "primeval sludge"? New insects and animals are being found by naturalists every year now.

How, too, did male and female occur in almost every animal, fish, bird and insect?

Scientists or evolutionists cannot prove their belief in a non-dinosaur ancestor for dinosaurs. Where then did they evolve from

The wonderfully complex and diverse living world around us will, I suppose, remain a source of awe and marvel for ever, and i remains true that neither Darwin's extremely complex, and detailed "scientific" book, nor any of the arguments therein go an way at all towards providing an answer to the very simple question–

"Where did that <u>second monkey</u> come from?"

The Old Testament was written over many centuries; the Ne Testament over several years.

The coming of Jesus Christ, who was the "SON OF GOD", gave us the choice to become Christians, or not, and the world ha changed as a result; but this change happened bit by bit, and perso by person.

His "FATHER", who is GOD, made the world, and everythi and everyone on it. All are perfect and unique!

This seems to be incredible, I agree, but it is much more credible than the theories advanced by Darwin. How else did the unimaginable marvels we see all around us come into being? Wh other Force has been powerful enough? Where did the untold multitudes of stars and planets appear from?

ONLY GOD IS WONDERFUL ENOUGH AND MIGHTY ENOUGH TO ACCOMPLISH THESE MARVELLOUS THINGS!

A SPECTACULAR MIRACLE!

The Transformation of a Caterpillar into A Butterfly

Anything more unlike a monkey is hard to imagine, but this picture is important as well.

The delicate wings of a butterfly, as it hovers over an open flower, or sits on a twig, are spectacular! Then, separate tinges of blue and green seem to melt into one glorious patch of incandescence as the little creature takes off and floats up into the air. Quite different from a squirrel and entirely unlike any monkey or ape!

This is just one more example of why it is impossible for all of these animals to have emerged from a swamp (or any other such material, primeval or not!), no matter how many thousands or even millions of years might have passed since their creation.

As I admire these exquisite animals and insects, I have to reflect, too, about the methods used by scientists and naturalists as they estimate the age of the world- or anything else in God's creation! Carbon dating, which is one method, seems to bc fine for calculating the age of anything under the age of about five thousand years or so, but it becomes more and more inaccurate after that period. It must be, therefore, wildly inaccurate, used as it has been.

Let us return to the bible, and the truth in its pages! The sun, moon and stars were made in order to provide light and warmth and to give us day and night. Then, on the fifth and sixth days, God created the sea creatures, birds and animals- each perfectly formed, and complete.

After all of this, the wonder of men and women came into being- as we have explored already.

Genesis 1:31 sums it all up for us – "God saw all that He had made, and it was very good."

Where, then, is our poor, shivering, single monkey struggling bit by bit out of the sludge? It seems to be extremely spurious, and really impossible compared with the Glory which we find in Genesis!

It is so dreadful that people – the perfect creation of God- have made such a mess of things! Our world at the present time is hovering on the brink of a precipice.

All of this is incredible, and many of us struggle to understand or make some sense of what we hear, see, and experience around us today. The truth is, however, that God did <u>not</u> just abandon us all to our feeble struggles! In the New Testament is revealed the biggest miracle of all time! Matthew chapter 1, verses 22 to 23, tells us what that was. <u>All this took place to fulfill what the Lord has said through the prophet – over six hundred years earlier –</u>

"The virgin will be with child, and will give birth to a son, and they will call him Immanuel"- which means "God with us".

Jesus, the "Son of God" (as John's Gospel chapter 1 verse 34 proclaims), achieved the impossible- He was born of a woman and grew up to be the "Saviour of the whole world".

This child was no half-formed, shivering creature, still to be completed over the course of time by the addition of a gut or a muscle!

What about the first woman, though? How did she come into being? Again, we are left in no doubt at all about that!

In Genesis chapter 2, verse 31, the story is completed, where it says, "So then God caused the man to fall into a deep sleep, and, while he was sleeping, He took one of the man's ribs, and closed up the place with flesh. Then the Lord God made a woman from the rib He had taken out of the man, and He brought her to the man."

Adam must have been completely overcome by the beauty and perfection of this wondrous creation of God!

Again, this is something incredible; but so very different to what Darwin and his followers believed.

I am sure that I can hear my reader say – <u>"that is totally impossible!"</u>

But – Is it any more impossible to believe that we were created by chance over countless millions of years?

To me, "The march of progress" is not needed after all!

What about the rest of what we see around us?

First of all, God created the heavens and the earth

(Genesis 1: 1)

Was that what the "BIG BANG," so loved by scientists, was all about?

Then day and night came into being. (Genesis 3-5)

Next, there was the creation of the seas and dry land. (Genesis 1:5-10), and then vegetation, plants and trees – so vital for our existence were created (Genesis 1:11-13).

From the probabilities of Darwin, we must turn to the Truth of the Bible. Then, we do not have to search very far to find now God brought about this, as it is found in the very first book of the Old Testament – Genesis.

In Genesis chapter 1, verse 26, we find the words - then God said, "Let us make man in our image, in our likeness." God then did just that! There is no ambiguity here! Everything is set out plainly and succinctly.

If we wonder how God accomplished the miracle of creation, we are left in no doubt at all. Genesis 2 verse 7 tells us that "The Lord God formed the man from the dust of the ground and breathed into his nostrils the breath of life, and the man became a living being."

Everything is set out, almost mathematically, as God acts in His wisdom and His power. Who has not stood amazed – staring at the incredible wonder and majesty of the pinks, reds, blues and purples of a wonderful sunrise or sunset- something that we, as human beings, could never emulate, however hard we try.

If there are young parents reading these pages today – how often have you been transfixed as you have gazed down at a tiny baby – either at her mother's breast or fast asleep in her tiny cot? How can such tiny life have come into this world? How was it possible for her to be immersed in amniotic fluid one minute and ı breathe air like any adult the next? This miracle beats any posed monkey by miles!!

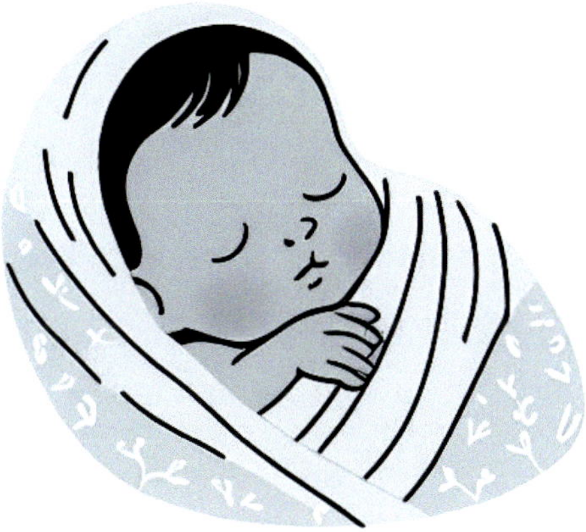

Do any of you people who have waded patiently through these es know why we were created? What was the purpose for ch God bothered to create us?"

Once again, the Bible has the perfect answer for us! Once in, all we have to do is to look in the New Testament, where esians chapter 2 verse 10 tells us that "we are God's kmanship, created in Christ Jesus, to do good works, which d prepared in advance for us to do."

Our God, whom so many see as indifferent and uncaring, ha said – in Isaiah 43 –

“He who created you …….

He who formed you…………

I have summoned you by name; you are mine: since you are precious and honoured in my sight, and because I love you!”

God continues to speak to each one of us in verse 25 of that same chapter –

“I, even I, am He who blots out your transgressions, for my own sake, and who remembers your sins no more.”

(Transgressions and sins are all the rotten things you almost certainly have done, and now just cannot forgive yourself for!).

Perhaps, as you are reading these words, you are sniggering quietly to yourself, saying:

“All of that is just nonsense! It is not for me!”

I myself, however, can appreciate fully now that the Bible i true! Even though; in previous times I did read the Bible sometimes, I missed completely the truths contained in its pages To me, the world was an unkind and forbidding place, as I struggled to see how someone as unloved and worthless as myse could be worthy of the attention of a God so perfect and holy.

The day came when this all changed completely, and I remember it vividly!

Let me digress for a while at this point – I shall come back it shortly!

LITTLE MIRACLES OF GOD'S CREATION.

Now to a much lighter and colourful subject – one which I shall introduce with a picture of Scottish red squirrels. I think these wonderful creatures are among the most beautiful and delicate of God's creation, and yet they are able to climb up (or down) the tallest trees, seemingly without any effort at all.

When people introduced grey squirrels into Britain, they did not care that their careless action would decimate our native red squirrel population. They would out-compete the reds for food, but, most serious of all, they brought the deadly disease of squirrel pox with them, which the reds cannot withstand.

Why red squirrels? Purely because my wife and I loved them so much, and it is so easy to see God's handiwork in their beauty.

They can bring us to a place of worship as we wonder at the complexity and beauty of these creatures.

They are "little miracles" of God's creation!

We tend to turn away, however, because it is so easy today to look at the newspaper headlines and then to wonder:

"Where is God in the terrible mess that we see around us daily?"

But God is very much still here! It is the actions of men and women, not of God, which have brought about the terrible state of the world - in the same way that thoughtless people brought disease and death to our red squirrel population!

Take time now to wonder at God's handiwork, and let that lead you into God's presence. Turn to the New Testament, and allow the Truth in its pages to bring you to a realisation that the words you reading are as relevant today as they ever were.

God spoke to me in the midst of pain and confusion as I struggled miserably and alone in the mire of depression and self-condemnation.

In the book of Romans, chapter 1, in verse 20, these words leap out from the pages – "For since the creation of the world God's ____eternal power and divine nature have been clearly seen, being understood from what has been made, so that men and women are without excuse."

I was totally taken aback by this, but there is more! Chapter 8, verse 1 spoke clearly to me. "Therefore, there is now no condemnation for those in Christ Jesus, because through Jesus

Christ the law of the Spirit of life set me free from the law of sin and death."

As I struggled in my very own "primeval swamp", these truths were a revelation to me. Years earlier, I had taken the step of "giving my life to Jesus Christ", but everything had gone wrong, and certainly, I did not feel either good or "saved".

Now I saw clearly that, even though I keep on doing what I do not want to do, and never seem to be able to do the things I really want to do - as Romans chapter 7, verse 17 confirms: "It is no longer I myself who do it, but it is sin living in me."

God loves us, even though we fail in so many ways, and, as verse 31 states, "If God is for us, who can be against us!"

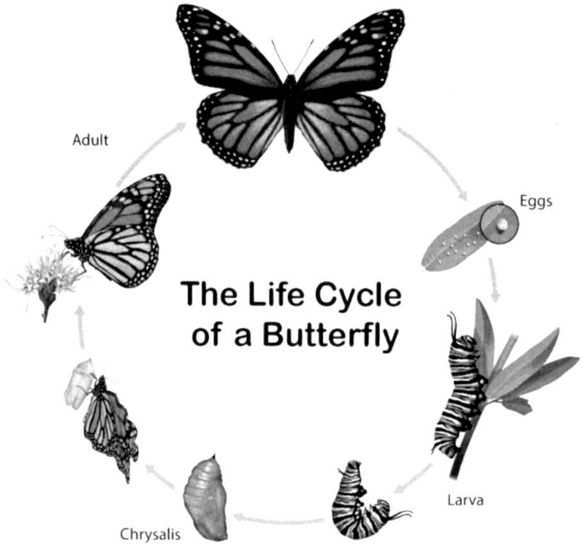

My readers may be wondering – "How is it possible that we can be sure that God loves us and will never leave us?"

The New Testament will tell us! We have only to look.

John 3:16 says, "God loved the people of this world so much that He gave his only Son so that everyone who has faith in Him will have eternal life, and never die."

Why do you think it is that we do not seem to succeed in living as God wants us to? Why do we continue to do wrong, and allow our "sins" to get us into all kinds of trouble?

This sad state of affairs is confirmed In Romans 3:23, where it says, "All of us have sinned, and fall short of the glory of God."

There is only one hope for all of us who struggle but fail to live "***good lives***", and that is "through the redemption that came by Jesus Christ." (Romans 3:24). That is the only way!

Revelation 3:20 says, "Here I am! I stand at the door and knock. If anyone hears my voice and opens the door, I will come in and eat with him, and he with me."

It is not, however, so simple as that. It is necessary, in addition, to do one more thing. TO ACCEPT JESUS CHRIST, and PUT OUR LIFE IN HIS CARE, and there is a very simple prayer which you could just say to Jesus Christ in order to do just that:

"Lord Jesus, I am sorry that I have not been going your way, but have tried to make my life work in my own way. Thank you that you died on the cross for me. Please change me; be first in my life in every way from now on, and make me into the kind of person you want me to be."

Having prayed this prayer, it is certain that Jesus Christ has heard it, so that you are now His son or daughter, that things can never be the same in your life from now on, and you can begin to experience life with God as He wanted from the beginning,

Perhaps you feel different after having prayed that prayer, but not every person will experience this. That is entirely OK, and, bit by bit, you will find that your life does change.

Trust in God and Jesus Christ as your Saviour, read your Bible, and pray to Him every day, remembering what the Bible affirms in Romans 8 verses 38 and 39.

"For I am convinced that neither death nor life, neither angels nor demons, neither the present nor the future, nor any powers, neither height nor depth nor anything else in all creation, will be able to separate us from the love of God that is in Christ Jesus our Lord."

THAT IS TRUTH FOR YOU FROM NOW ON!

Lies And The Truth

At the age of eighty-five, I regret that I am no longer able to go for long walks in the beautiful Scottish mountains and hills.

As a younger man, I would often go for a hike around Deeside or the Cairngorms, sometimes even spending a night camping out. In spring, summer, autumn or winter, these hills are exceedingly beautiful and have an endless magnetism, whatever the weather.

Over the years I have explored these endlessly exciting uplands, I can count on the fingers of one hand the number of times I have glimpsed Scotland's only poisonous snake – the adder. This beautiful snake is very shy and prefers to hide from any human presence.

When you do see them, it makes up for all the other times! They come in various colours, with black, brown or white jagged stripes and many different colours. If you stand quietly and do not disturb them, they will continue their activities until they decide to slither off into the undergrowth.

Why am I talking about snakes?

The Bible introduces this reptile very early on – in Genesis chapter 3, verse 1, it says, "The serpent was more crafty than any of the wild animals the Lord God had made."

This snake, by innuendo and lies, induced, first of all, Eve and then Adam, to ignore the word of God- He told them that they "must not eat the fruit of the tree that is in the middle of the garden" of Eden. Instead "when the woman saw that the fruit of the tree was good for food, and pleasing to the eye, and also desirable for gaining wisdom, she took some and ate it. She also gave some to her husband, who was with her, and he ate it."

Of course, the snake was, in fact, Satan himself, and his soft, insidious lies led to disaster and chaos! Since then, human beings have faced all kinds of troubles, pains and suffering, and the world appears to be sliding ever faster into chaos and disastrous wars.

Today, he is still every bit as busy, and his temptations seem to be everywhere around us.

Now, men and women are faced daily with the same choices as Adam and Eve in the Garden of Eden:

Shall I go God's way today?

Shall I ignore what God says and take the "easy way", which the enemy is always speaking into my ear?

We must be very careful about this, however, because the second choice will lead us into chaos and darkness, pain, defeat, and, eventually, to what the Bible calls hell.

It has been many years since I made my mind up on this subject. My choice was to invite God into my life and to endeavour to go God's way, difficult as it has been at times.

Galatians chapter 5, verse 1 shows that we all have an entirely free choice in this:

"It is for freedom that Christ has set us free. Stand firm, then, and do not let yourself be burdened again by a yoke of slavery."

I shall finish this book now with the words of Ephesians chapter 1: - "For (God) chose us……. before the world's creation to be holy and blameless in His sight. In love, He predestined us to be adopted as His sons and daughters through Jesus Christ……….

In Him, we have redemption through His blood, the forgiveness of sins, in accordance with the riches of God's grace that He lavished on us with all wisdom and understanding."

The same chapter says, "God's power is like the working of His mighty strength, which He exerted in Christ when He raised Him from the dead and seated Him at His right hand in the heavenly realms."

Praise God that these things are true!

COULD IT BE THAT THE WORLD, FOR SO MANY DECADES, HAS BELIEVED IN LIES, RATHER THAN IN GOD?

About The Author

Colin Neave was born in Aberdeen, Scotland, in 1939 and, except for eight years, has lived in Aberdeenshire up until now. In 1963, he married Annette and, in due course, their daughter and son were born.

Later both Annette and Colin became trained and experienced counsellors, spending much of their time supporting and counselling others. In 2015, Colin Published a book called "Scriptural Healing and Wholeness", sharing his insights about the necessity of basing our lives on the absolute truth contained in scripture.

They travelled widely together, teaching and counselling in many different countries, with a particular focus on Northern Macedonia, where their work touched countless lives all over that country.

In September 2024, Colin faced an immense personal loss when Annette died after suffering from dementia for four years. Her death was a tremendous blow, marking the end of their remarkable partnership, but leaving behind a legacy of compassion, faith and dedication.